BRIEFI

GW01019440

The Poorest of the Poor?

The peoples of the West African Sahel

Glenn Myers

OM
publishing

Copyright © 1998 Glenn Myers

First published 1998 by OM Publishing

OM Publishing is an imprint of Paternoster Publishing,
P.O. Box 300, Carlisle, Cumbria, CA3 0QS, U.K.

03 02 01 00 99 98   7 6 5 4 3 2 1

British Library Cataloguing in Publication Data
A catalogue record for this book is available from the British Library

ISBN 1-85078-299-7

Designed by Christopher Lawther, Teamwork, Lancing, West Sussex.
Typeset by WestKey Ltd, Falmouth, Cornwall.
Produced by Jeremy Mudditt Publishing Services, Carlisle,
and printed and bound in Great Britain by WEC Press, Gerrards Cross, Bucks.

CONTENTS

This book was produced from the International Research and UK Publications
departments of WEC International.

WEC International is an interdenominational missions agency aiming to bring
the Christian gospel to the remaining unevangelised peoples of the world.
WEC has over 1850 workers from 43 nations serving together in 60 countries.

Start here

This book describes the challenges for the Church in West Africa.

We look at this whole region because it gives us the vital scene-setting and the economic context for the part of West Africa we're really interested in: the region highlighted on the map and usually called the 'West African Sahel'.

'Sahel' is the Arabic for 'shore'. The Sahel is the southern 'shore' of the Sahara desert. Most of the peoples who live here are Muslim. The rest follow African Traditional Religion. Together they make up one of those few remaining worlds in which Christ is yet to be really known, loved, or worshipped – one of the last great unclimbed peaks for the gospel.

Many people helped on this project. Almost all of them are committed in one way or another to serving the peoples of the Sahel. Special thanks to:

John & Margaret Bardsley
Colin & Jean Bearup
Hans & Elfi Bohl
Nick Burn
Shord van Donge
Reuben Ezemadu
Jean-Marc Fritsch
Martin Jennings
Patrick & Robyn Johnstone
Knox & Shona Haggie
Lamin Kanté
Anne Kelland
David Maranz
Jeremy Mudditt
Emmanuel Olewa
David Phillips
Richard Shawyer
Daphne Spraggett
Larry Vanderaa
André Wenk

Thanks to those organizations and individuals whose work I've quoted. I tried to locate the copyright owners for the longer pieces but did not always succeed; I hope to be able to put that right in any future editions of this book.

Thanks too to other colleagues in the mission I work for, WEC International, for their contribution in various ways to this ongoing series. WEC's International Research Office patiently put together the research files that are the basis of this book. WECers also supplied the photos.

. . . and of course extra-special thanks to Cordelia and our children.

Glenn Myers
Cambridge, 1998.

– 1 –
Land

THE HOT HOUSE

Welcome to the hot house, an exuberant place that makes the so-called temperate lands like Northern Europe look dank, chilly, small and grey.

West Africa apparently orders its climate in bulk loads, buying in petawatts of sunshine that barbecue the land for months on end; and fat rainclouds that burst over the dry soil like end-of-season fruit.

The deep Sahara, where the sun has been known to shine every day for six years at a stretch, is about the driest part of the world. Lengths of the West African coast are some of the wettest. Between the two extremities the landscape is divided into horizontal strips that turn greener as you move south: first, stony desert; then scrubland; then areas of savannah grass and baobab trees; and

finally the West African bush and patches of rainforest. The greener the strip, the longer the rains.

A TOUGH PLACE

You have to be clever to live here.

Most West Africans are farmers. And consider what it's like to farm, for example, a patch of one of the browner, northern strips. Starting with poor topsoil, some seeds, your own hands, no capital, and under orders from your father or husband you must:

- Coax a year's nutrition for your family from the sand, using only millet and cassava, and with no rain whatsoever for eight months of the year

- Build or maintain a home using only the elements you can dig up or find around you

- Supply all your water needs

- Find enough spare cash to buy the food that you can't grow; the medicines your children will need; the loans your family and friends will require of you; and for enough votive offerings to keep a host of hungry evil spirits, ancestors, and senior spiritual beings off your back.

A WORLD AWAY

I give a lesson about life in England to the oldest class in the [Burkina Faso] village school. This produces some lively interest – and some illuminating questions . . . How do you hunt? How do you keep animals? How do you eat? Do you fetch wood for your fire? Do you have wells? What do children wear to school? Do you have Peulh (nomadic pastoralists)? Do you have black people? Are black people accepted by white people? Do you carry babies on your backs like we do?[1]

ONLY SLIGHTLY EASIER

Only slightly easier is foraging for wealth in the cities. Every possible way of making a living in urban areas is already mined to exhaustion.

A vanful of grown men will turn up on your doorstep to take one reading of the electricity meter. In the markets you will find rows of identical tables offering precisely the same stock for sale at exactly the same price: no unexploited market niches here. Outside the markets, you will find people who buy meat scraps or exercise books from the markets to sell them to anybody who doesn't fancy the walk to town.

Every shopkeeper, truck owner, building contractor or tradesman will be surrounded by a squadron of apprentices, labourers, gophers, and assorted hangers-on – extended family members usually. These people share out the work when there is any, sit around until the shade moves when there isn't, and eat together at the end of the day, one wage stretched out among them all. Disabled and mentally handicapped family members, and widows and orphans, are also all fed from the same family pot – a fact both remarkable and sad.

Wherever there is the faintest whisper of wealth, a large group of people will be chasing it. An education really only opens up the chance to work in government service; but there are too many educated people chasing too few jobs. An Islamic education may lead to a career in a foreign-funded Muslim school; but again, there's oversupply of scholars.

IT ALL DEPENDS

What you make of these hardships depends rather on whose perspective you use.

If you look through the lens of the United Nations' measures of development you may only see overwhelming poverty. Half of the world's poorest two-dozen countries are West African; of those, three of the poorest five are the Sahelian states of Burkina Faso, Mali and Niger.[2] That means babies die when they don't need to; people are malnourished; life choices are few.

It's different if you look at the area, for example, from the viewpoint of an ethnic group that is key to this whole book: the Fulbe. (Also known, depending where you find them, as Fula, Fulani, Peul, and by many other names).

These people walk with their herds hundreds of miles between traditional Sahelian pasture lands each year, tramping north in the rainy season, south in the dry, looking out for grass and avoiding the tsetse fly. Like the Israelites in the desert, they carry everything with them as they go.

As for as the Fulbe are concerned, the rigours of the Sahel sort out the real men (them) from everyone else. They are proud to have ruled this vast area over the centuries, conquering both its other inhabitants and its pepper-hot climate. When it comes to living rightly, they believe, nobody does it better. On the canvas of the Sahel, the Fulbe have painted every value that matters: courage, skill, steadfastness, toughness, simple living, generosity.

The principle holds throughout West Africa. Even an outsider cannot help being proud to belong to the same human species as West Africa's enterprising families of farmers, herders and traders. They are creating life and societies out of almost nothing, and sharing the little they have with a generosity most of us cannot fathom. Only in material terms are they the poorest of the poor.

THE CHRISTIAN CHURCH

Into this stark world, the Church has the job of bringing the gospel. The job is only partially complete.

West Africa's Christian community is stripey, like the land. The nearer you get to the desert, the fewer the Christians are. Ghana, on the coast, is 44% Christian (counting all

> *If you spend yourself on behalf of the hungry,*
> *and satisfy the needs of the oppressed,*
> *then your light will rise in the darkness,*
> *and your night will become like noonday.*
> *The Lord will guide you always;*
> *he will satisfy your needs in a sun-scorched land.*[3]

who in the broadest sense would claim some kind of allegiance to Christ); its northern neighbour Burkina Faso is 13% Christian; Burkina's northern neigh-bour Mali, a Sahara-desert state, is only 2% Christian.[4] This reflects mission history in West Africa: work has been concentrated on the animist, bush-dwelling farmers rather than the Muslim, desert- and savannah-roaming nomads.

These little-touched northern strips are home to a continent's worth of different ethnic groups. The 'Joshua Project 2000 List' is a list of all the peoples on earth who are more than 10,000 in population and less than 3% evangelical or 5% total Christian. It counts more than 350 such peoples in West Africa. Mostly, these are the peoples of the northern strips, the peoples of the Sahel.

I WANT TO GET OFF

Rapid change and great stress further confuse the scene. This is a period in history in which the cultures of the Sahel are being ploughed up. Droughts are one part of the cause, the collision with the modern world is another.

Here are some observations from elderly villagers in Mali. The climate problems first:

'Nature is not as generous as it used to be.'

'Today the sky turns red from the colour of dust and sand - there is no rain.'

'Fishing yesterday and today are two different things. Yesterday you went to fish in lakes, but today you have to fish in your pocket.'

And then the cultural issues:

'Today, if you want to get married you walk around with a head full of problems.'

'In the old days your child was everybody's child.'

'In the past the whole family, from all over the village, had a say in a child's education.'

'Today only parents are responsible for their children's upbringing; before, the whole community was concerned.'

'These days it seems as though the children are bringing up the adults!'[5]

THIS BOOK

The worldwide Church owes it to the peoples of the Sahel to bring them the gospel, in this period of history, whatever the costs or difficulties. In the following pages I have tried to describe what the job is like. I have drawn heavily on the thoughts and perspectives of foreign and local evangelical Christians who are working in, or for, the region.

THE PROBLEM OF 'POOR'

Here's the dilemma.

My son, born in wealthy Singapore, was, according to the statistics, 99.5% certain to survive his first year. A little boy born on the same day among Fulbe nomadic pastoralists in Mali was only 89% likely to reach his first birthday.[6] To put it another way, for every five Singaporean baby-deaths, there are over a hundred Malian ones.

How can anyone make sense of this injustice? Why is West Africa poor?

First, the word 'poor' is unfortunate. It is a pity that in the English language 'poor' means 'deficient', 'lacking', 'second-rate' as well as simply 'not rich'. By describing West Africa as 'poor' we demean it. As we explain in the main text, living the 'poor' lifestyle requires both skill and character. You have to be smart and hardworking to make it as a peasant or a nomad.

Second, the peoples of West Africa are only as 'poor' as most people everywhere have been through history. Instead of describing them as 'poor' you could equally well call their self-sufficient, rural existence 'normal'. The farmers and nomads of West Africa typify the modal, standard forms of human existence through the centuries. The richer countries are the unusual ones.

A better question

A better question might be 'Why are some parts of the world rich and others not?'

Is it that:

- The rich world has exploited the poor parts?

- The poor world has natural disadvantages over the rich parts when it comes to creating wealth?

The answer to both questions is 'Yes' but the reality is still more complicated. Countries are scattered evenly all along a scale between 'richest' and 'poorest'. They are all in motion relative to each other, coping well or badly with a world that changes every day. All sin and all exploit each other. All are lifted up and laid low by God. Today's snapshot reality is temporary. People in the West or the developed East won't be agonizing about their relative wealth forever.

And other snapshots would show a different scene. The Sahara, for example, has not always been a desert. Nomads of the Sahel have at times controlled great wealth (as we shall see in Chapter 3). Africans once made up part of a modern army, garrisoned in murky climes near Carlisle in the north of England, that subdued the primitive British tribes two thousand years ago.[7] And today's superpower will be tomorrow's basket-case unless history is switched off at midnight.

None of the Christian workers I asked could really answer the 'why' questions about poverty and riches, even though they lived with the dilemmas of them every day. I got the impression that, practical people as they are, they preferred to ask themselves the 'What' question:

'What does the Lord require of you?'

. . . and they would all of course endorse the prophet Micah's answer:

'To act justly and to love mercy and to walk humbly with your God.'[8]

– 2 –
Culture

We can't hope to understand the real issues involved in taking the gospel to the Sahel unless we spend some time looking at people's mindset, or 'worldview'.

You may find the climate and landscape of the Sahel strange and even hostile. That's nothing, compared with the alien territory we stumble over when we look at the spiritual and cultural 'geography' of the region.

We look at just three features of this Sahelian mindset:

- Working with spirits
- Sharing resources
- Sticking to tradition

WORKING WITH SPIRITS

In the Sahel, spiritual forces matter. Coping with them is at least as important to most people as coping with the tax and benefit systems in our own countries is to us.

A Nigerian brother told me, 'You see, we Africans, we can never have an atom of doubt about spiritual powers. You understand – we were born in it . . . We can't doubt the presence of demons and their working.'

Words that for many of us belong to fairy tales[1] – 'sorcery', 'magic', 'spells' for example – describe vital realities, things real enough to consider having a career in them.

Not only is this true, but this world-system, just like the standard Western one, works – in part. In part, through a glass darkly, it explains what is going on and why things happen.

We find this so hard to believe that it is worth looking at in more detail. For example, why – you might ask – did a soccer player miss the vital kick in a penalty shoot-out at the end of a match? Was it:

1 He was tired and mis-hit his shot
2 'It wasn't to be.'

One answer looks for a modern, Western solution – the angle of the boot was wrong, because his blood-sugar levels were low, and he wasn't thinking clearly.

The other answer suggests that somehow, outside forces decided the final score. He was destined to miss; his team were fated to lose. What was the real reason for final result: was it fitness or fate? Should the player have trained harder or should the team have called in a shaman? There's the shape of the two world-views.

And both types of worldview make a reasonable shot (forgive the pun) at 'really' answering the questions. Each worldview has its strengths but neither one is obviously right in all circumstances.

For example, when asked, 'Why did my daugher get malaria?' the Western doctor says that a mosquito carrying the malaria parasite bit her. End of question. But the African then asks the question that really matters to him: 'Yes, but who sent the mosquito?'

Look at these questions:

• Why has she fallen in love with him, and not with me?

- Why have our cattle fallen sick? (and not yours)
- How can I protect my child from harm?

Here, the Western worldview might offer a few simple platitudes – and then fall silent. African worldviews will engage and tackle all this.

DIFFERENT WORLDVIEW, DIFFERENT WORLD

> **THE MARABOUT'S APPRENTICE – I**
> Uncle had a lot of power. He performed all the sacrifices which the demons require for their services. He had a special contract with a demon called S— -. Before he could communicate with him he slaughtered a he- and a she-goat for him. It was all accompanied by a lot of rituals. My uncle had to renew the contract every year. If not, the demon would kill his younger brother or another member of his family. He himself would go crazy.[2]

This leads directly to different ways of living life, different priorities for solving problems, different calls on people's cash. Pacifying, manipulating, and fending off forces from the spiritual realm is a big industry in the Sahel.

The Wolof language, spoken by most people in Senegal, for example, has at least 49 different words for different spiritual specialities, for example:

- *Priest*: performs regular rituals

- *Prophet*: delivers personal messages and works miracles

- *Shaman*: receives personal communication from a supernatural being, over which he has some control or mastery

- *Diviner*: makes a diagnosis of problems, for example by taking readings of cowrie shells.

Spiritual forces are carefully ranked and classified. Everyone from the smallest child will know who the local ruling spirit is. Shamans will deal with a couple of higher-order spiritual beings (often called 'divinities'), as well as with dozens of lower-order demons. Political leaders hire experts who can help them get advice from, say, the god of the Moon. Fallen angels are alive, well, and publicly active in this region.

You can invest in spells or procedures for many human conditions: love spells; sorcery to call family members home from the cities; charms to protect against spiritual attack. Anthropologist David Maranz told me that he was once offered six different spells for clearing out fishbones that stuck in the throat. Four were for on-site use, two worked remotely.

Nor is this spiritual dabbling considered 'evil' by those who use it. The spirits themselves, for the most part, are thought to be morally neutral. Some of the magic is considered evil by its practitioners; but most is not. It's the African equivalent of playing the stockmarket: investors usually think it worthwhile in the long-term, but even the smartest sometimes lose their shirts (or their souls).

This is a small introduction to a large subject; but even from this we can imagine some of the consequences:

1 *High costs*. This spiritual activity is supported by the ordinary people of the region as yet another tax-on-living. Human beings are the ceremonial centre of the known universe, oiling the wheels of the natural order, tinkering with the engine of the cosmos to keep it ticking over properly. And it costs.

These spirits are easily affronted. You have to welcome new babies, marry, and bury old people with ceremony and expenses you can't afford. You have to make regular offerings. You have to tackle uncleanness and disharmony. Cities, for example, offer regular sacrifices to ruling spirits, perhaps a cow or a goat. Several different African sources told me that on occasions young children or strangers are also offered.

2 *Futility*. This spiritual world is a replica of the world the Bible describes in books like 1 and 2 Kings: ethnic groups mingled together, all trying out each others' gods and rituals to get ahead in life. Biblical prophets wailed and lamented over this whole outlook; God, they proclaimed, hates the whole exercise as utterly futile and destructive. It is right to believe in evil spirits and be wary of their power; but it's wrong to try to harness that power.

3 *The need for a Spirit-filled gospel*: Any gospel brought to the Sahel is no gospel at all unless it takes these powers seriously and can demonstrate an alternative that works, in the form of an uncompromising trust in Christ and a day-by-day living experience of the Holy Spirit.

A SHARING LIFE

A second deep principle for many people of the Sahel is that you share your life with the rest of your extended family, and in a sense with your whole ethnic group.

You look to your family and people, and not to the state, for social security and for employment. You find a marriage partner from your own group. No-one else, except your group, will stand up for your rights or defend your corner.

In return, if you do well, for example through getting a government job, it is a matter of honour that you use your position and wealth for the good of your own people. Outsiders may see that as nepotism; you see it as integrity and decency.

This instinctive solidarity leads to practices that seem most strange to many foreigners. Take money for example:[4]

- In Sahel Africa, passing money and help around is the stuff of friendship and family solidarity.[5] Friendship involves giving and receiving money.

- You must help your friends and family when they are in need, in the certainty that they will help you when you are in need.

- You can't be a true friend unless it touches your finances. Failure to be involved materially cannot be compensated for by anything else. You must share what you have.

- Keeping money in a bank, or having two radios when you need only one, is hoarding, especially when you have friends or family members who need the money or the resources.

- If you are rigorous in keeping track of money, that shows a mean spirit.

- If you budget, that too is mean.

- You should only approach someone to pay back a loan if you now need the money more than they do.

It is pointless to ask if these principles are 'better' or 'worse' than principles derived in Western contexts, any more than asking if a baobab is 'better' than an oak tree. Sahelian principles are rotten at creating wealth but great for surviving calamities. Western principles may be equally strong and weak in the opposite directions.

The challenge to cultural outsiders trying to bring the gospel is obvious:

1 *Confusion.* Anyone arriving in the Sahel from richer parts of the world is doomed to suffer confusing relationships with Africans of the Sahel wherever money is concerned. Your African friends will happily ask you for money, because you are their friend. How can a rich person be a true friend and not give away his money when his friends need it? What kind of a friend is that?

Yet faced with requests for money, a person from the rich world panics. He hates the sight of his friends begging him for money. He is terrified of the thought that he might be bribing people to accept the gospel. And his own mindset tells him that his money is really for his own little family's use.

2 *Commitment.* If Christians here are to call other people effectively to follow Christ, they must be prepared to make up for everything a convert will lose if his family oppose him. They must be prepared to be his security, to offer him food and shelter, to care for him when he is sick, even to find him a wife and a job.

African families do not usually reject people for ever, even if they turn to Christ from a Muslim or animist background. But in the painful interim when the convert is new and the family hostile, the church must bridge the gap, or, humanly speaking, the convert will fall.

STICKING TO TRADITION

Third, the societies we are focussing on in this book are not naturally eager to experiment with new ideas.

This is no bad thing either. We in the West are grateful that medical teams in operating theatres, for example, are not made up of creative, moody individualists. Life and death issues, like surviving in West Africa, demand leadership, discipline, teamwork; all things that African cultures are great at.

Fathers or grandfathers rule the family with authority. Before they die, they solemnly charge the next generation to maintain the family altar and traditions. Through centuries, this has been the way that the patterns of life deemed essential for survival have been kept up. So thin are the margins between life and death, you are not encouraged to experiment.

Tradition also applies to local ideas about health care. I asked a nurse who had worked in primary health care for ten years among West African Muslims what improvements she had seen in child health practices. 'Very little,' she replied. 'People change only slowly. Ask me again after 40 years.'

In the spiritual world, marabouts and other professionals learn early in their apprenticeship the need to pronounce spells and work through rituals in exactly the right format, for their own spiritual protection – a kind of health and safety at work.

THE POWER OF RITUAL

The same principle of sticking to the traditional rules goes some way to explain the power of ritual throughout these cultures.

All humans, of course, are involved in rituals at some time or other. Watch the way soccer captains never miss shaking hands at the beginning of a match, or the way you always go through the same greetings when you arrive at work. Here's the English version of this: 'Morning' 'Morning' 'How are you?' 'Fine'. We all use rituals to enforce the idea that, culturally and relationally, everything is OK.

And West African cultures are ritual-rich. You find rituals to ease each one of life's passages: becoming a person, becoming an adult, getting married, becoming a parent, becoming an ancestor. There are rituals for when the rains haven't come, or for when owls are eating your sick child's soul. Doing them feels deeply right; avoiding them is frightening. Changing them is a measure of real change in the depths. And by that measure, people are changing only slowly.

Early mission attempts to abolish certain rituals among Christianized people in West Africa only pushed the rituals underground. People would get married in the church-approved way, and then return quietly to the village for the traditional rites. Nowadays, religious movements are springing up in long-Christianized parts of the region, calling people back to the suppressed religions of the past.

All this means that anyone who wants to bring lasting change to a Sahelian culture is taking on a huge challenge. You must be able to demonstrate that the change is definitely for the better. You must be able to face the wrath of the local establishment if you can't carry them with you. And your teaching must have a breadth and depth that will make change rumble through the whole society, touching even the rituals.

Miss out this slowness, this thoroughness, aim 'just to go out for a couple of years and fix things', and you find that innovations of whatever kind are accepted only at the surface level; at the heart level they are dismissed. Witness the masses of rusting, broken-down tractors; the carefully built but unused clinics; or the so-called 'spiritual churches' that have a Christian shell but an unreformed, occult centre. All are examples of new ideas that have been outwardly adapted but never taken to heart.

THE CHALLENGE

Can the gospel flourish in these Sahelian landscapes of the mind? The answer is a certain Yes.

Acts 2:42–46 is often quoted as an example of what the Church should be like:

> *They devoted themselves to the apostles' teaching and to the fellowship,*
> *to the breaking of bread and to prayer. Everyone was filled with awe,*
> *and many wonders and miraculous signs were done by the apostles. All*
> *the believers were together and had everything in common. Selling their*
> *possessions and goods, they gave to anyone as he had need.*

This little snippet shows the gospel flourishing extraordinarily within a mindset similar in many ways to the Sahelian one:

- Spiritual power issues are addressed: there's prayer, awe, wonders and miracles.

- Sharing and security issues are addressed: by fellowship, holding everything in common, and selling possessions to support each other.

- Internalizing-truth issues are addressed: doctrine is taught thoroughly, and new rituals developed such as breaking bread and meeting together in the temple courts.

THE NEXT FRONTIER

Before we look at the actual current state of the Church in West Africa and the Sahel, we have to consider a further dominating presence among the peoples of the region: the long history and powerful appeal of Islam.

– 3 –
Islam

Over the last thousand years Islam has fused with local Sahelian cultures and is now as much a part of the scene here as ancient village parish churches are in the landscapes of Europe or Russia.

Where did West African Islam come from? And what is it like?

THE RULERS

Islam in West Africa started as a religion of the rulers and in the cities.

For the past millennium, the camel-owners (merchants, nomads, herders) have ruled both the Sahel and its farmers. These camel-owning elites met Islam when they carried their gold, slaves, and salt across the desert to the Arabs and Berbers in the north.

The Islam they encountered was modern, literate, confident, and expanding; simple, and yet a faith associated with the best science, art, architecture and empires they had ever seen.

Islamized Berbers subsequently conquered and ruled West Africa's first recorded great kingdom, Ghana (which was sited, confusingly, in modern-day Mali) in the 11th century. After that, Muslims dominated each of the Sahel's empires: the Kanem-Bornu around Lake Chad (Muslims were in charge from the tenth century all the way through to its 16th century peak and subsequently), the Malian empire (13th–14th century), the Songhai (15th–16th), and the Fulbe (18th–19th).

These empires were weighty enough for their leaders to get an occasional strut on the world stage. Mansa Musa, for example, ruled the Malian empire in the 14th century and dazzled for a time as the owner of the world's greatest gold mines. He made the pilgrimage to Mecca around 1324–25, visited Cairo as well, and spent lavishly wherever he went. He built Timbuktu, a Malian city on the shores of the Sahara, into a centre for Islamic learning and cross-desert trade.

THE MASSES

Through most of its West African history, Islam has only been the faith of the aristocracy. The turning of the masses happened after the conquests of Islamic reformers and European colonizers.

The Islamic reformers were eighteenth- or nineteenth-century figures, military leaders and politicians, as well as scholars and mystics, rather in the model of the prophet Muhammad himself.

Usman dan Fodio was the most famous. A Pullo[1] scholar and marabout, he overthrew his own Islamic rulers and then waged a war across the Sahel to the Hausa empire of Northern Nigeria.

HOW THE BIAFATAS TURNED

The Islamic reform movements made the Fulbe people in particular notable as zealous missionaries of Islam, with a wide effect all over West Africa.

In what is now the tiny state of Guinea-Bissau, for example, a century ago, nomadic Fulbe raided the Biafatas, a small, animist, farming tribe who number today about 30,000 people, the size of a small town. Among other things, they carried off a small boy whom they made a Pullo.

This boy, Daniel-like, excelled in his learning of the Fulbe ways and of Islam. Much later, he was banished from the Fulbe and he returned to his own people. Recognizing his abilities, and his usefulness in fighting off the Fulbe, they made him king. He agreed, on the grounds that the Biafatas became Muslims; and so they did and in this kind of way, among many others, Islam spread.

Around the same time as Europe was fighting the Napoleonic wars, Usman's cavalry were gathering year by year in the sun-bleached city of Sokoto, planning fresh incursions across West Africa. Though considered by many an Islamic hero, Usman shed blood by the bucketful and enslaved hundreds of thousands of people in his campaigns. Usman's empire lasted a century and reached to the fringes of the rainforest, islamizing wherever it went.

Its echo is still heard today. Many West African peoples date their islamization to this period. And the Fulbe/Hausa people still dominate the politics and religious outlook of Nigeria.

Umar Tal was another Islamic reformer. A marabout like Usman, Umar Tal conquered much of Mali and parts of Senegal, often compiling a list of theological reasons for attacking his fellow Muslims before he set out.

The flow to Islam continued when the European colonists took over. The reasons for this are complex: Traditional Religion was collapsing, and people were flowing both to Islam and Christianity. In Nigeria, for example, during the 20th century, Islam moved from claiming perhaps 20–25% of the population to today's 45–50%. Senegal is now over 90% Muslim: most of its Islamic growth happened under Western rule or during the current independence in which French influence remains very strong.

WHAT IS IT LIKE?

To understand West African Islam, we do well to forget everything we learnt in religious education classes at school.

Even if Islam were ever the neat package of beliefs served up in school textbooks (which it is not) its passage over the cultural landscape of the Sahel and through the centuries has totally reshaped it.

In particular it's:

- A learned behaviour
- Blended with African Traditional Religion.

A LEARNED BEHAVIOUR

Islam as practised in the Sahel is a set of rituals into which you are brought up.

Traditionally, it belongs to the realm of things that you don't question, like the fact that you belong to a certain people, or that you are a certain gender, or that you always cook meat before you eat it.

A Muslim is something you just *are*. And – especially if you belong to a people who are completely or almost completely Muslim – ceasing to be one is unthinkable. You may be a bad Muslim, even an awful one, but your community will tolerate you. However, if you cease to be a Muslim, you activate the tribal immune system. You may be bullied, expelled, even killed.

It almost needs a revelation from God for people to realize that things don't have to be this way: that you can be a Pullo or a Wolof, be truly part of the ethnic group, fulfill your obligations to your people, and yet not be a Muslim.

Further, you are not trained in most cases to think critically about your faith. The Qur'an is to be recited, not explored. You might find a Senegalese man praying a hundred times a day, with the help of beads, the lovely Sufi prayer, 'I take refuge in God . . . it is You we adore', yet he is typically speaking an Arabic chant taught him by his marabout, without necessarily thinking it out.

BLENDED WITH AFRICAN TRADITIONAL RELIGION

Then, Islam, and especially the brand of Islam that is found throughout the Sahel, reinforces and strengthens the old African Traditional worldviews.

Like Islam, African Traditional Religion is monotheistic, not polytheistic. It believes in one, high, all-powerful God but this God is remote, missing, not answering the phone. African Traditional Religions have stories as to why exactly the High God moved off the scene: our forefathers used to carry their spears upright, some will tell you, and they accidentally poked God and annoyed him.

Again, in African Traditional Religion, all the real work of celestial government is done by God's civil service, the spiritual beings, ancestors and other sources of power. They can be persuaded to get on your case if you supply an appropriate donation or sacrifice.

Much of this outlook slips easily enough into Islam. In Islam, too, God has a civil service, the 'angels' and the 'jinn'. Sometimes turning from African Traditional Religion to Islam is as simple as renaming 'the river-god' 'the river-jinn'.[2] (Though other times it is more of a problem – see the box.)

A PRIESTESS CONVERTS

One Friday in 1991 Bia Gomez walked into a large mosque in Banjul, the capital of the Gambia. This unkempt, pig-keeping, middle-aged woman was reputed to be the priestess of one of the greatest African Traditional Religion idols in Banjul.

People held her in awe. It was said that an idol from the nearby country of Guinea-Bissau had sent a spirit direct to Bia, in the form of whirlwind right outside her home.

Via an interpreter, Bia told the 2000-strong congregation that she was going to convert to Islam. Over the past several nights, she explained, two figures clad in white had come to her. They had forced her through long hours to bow, bend her knees, prostrate herself in prayers, in an exact copy of the way Muslims pray. If she got it wrong, or rebelled, these spirits stared at her and terrified her. Finally she had given in and decided to become a Muslim.

As she finished her story, the congregation began chanting 'God is great.' She was welcomed into the Islamic community, bathed, dressed in white, and given some small gifts to commemorate her conversion.

It is not unusual for people who follow African Traditional Religions to become Muslims. But Bia had been picked out by the spirits as special. Her family saw her conversion as a breach of sacred tradition. They tried to make her renounce Islam.

She was forced to leave home. Still her relatives pursued her, and, worn out by the trauma, Bia died shortly afterwards, only to spark off a fresh conflict as to how she was to be buried. Muslims saw her conversion as a confirmation of the traditional Islamic teaching that 'Islam will triumph in the end.'[3]

Islam then adds some extra 'value':

- It provides more information about the missing High God, what he wants from people, and how to get God's blessing now and in the hereafter.

- It links your local religious practice with another 'high faith' that is accepted all around the world, a sort of spiritual credit card, essential for the modern world.

- It offers new ways of accessing power through a magic book, and magic sayings and rituals.

This last point is so important. The Islam of the Sahel, just like the Traditional Religion of the Sahel, fusses over power for living. Islamics scholar Bill Musk has described how this so-called 'folk Islam' works:

- In folk Islam, the Qur'an is not studied for its meaning so much as used for magic. How did God create life? By sowing the world with the Qur'an. How do you cure sickness? Write some Qur'anic verses on a slate, wash them off and drink them. How do you protect against evil? Carry a Qur'anic text in a little leather bag around your neck.

- The confession, 'There is no god but God and Muhammad is his prophet', is used as a kind of spell to protect yourself when you walk into evil-feeling places.

- Alms are used either to save yourself from the evil eye that a beggar might put upon you; or as cash to donate to your local marabout as a kind of spiritual life insurance.

- Pilgrimage becomes a way of juicing yourself up with vital life force, 'baraka'. Muslims in Senegal will even prefer their own pilgrimage sites – the biggest is in the town of Touba – to the official ones in Mecca and Medina.

This folk Islam, then, has grown to fit the West African context beautifully. The result is a faith that is often poorly understood but passionately defended, as a matter of family or tribal honour; a faith whose rigours, such as the fast, appeal to the tough and brave peoples of the semi-desert; a faith that offers world-class spiritual power and influence as a supplement to the local deities; a faith that doesn't encourage you to think critically; and a faith that it is culturally very hard to leave behind completely.

If you are wanting to gain a hearing for the kindness and love of God in Christ, these are formidable barriers. Here's the testimony of a well-respected Christian missionary in Mali:

> *Sometimes I sit behind the mosque in our village when the men go for their evening prayers. At those moments Islam seems to me like an unmovable wall. How will these men, on the surface so united and sure in their beliefs, break ranks with their history, with their peers, with their leaders, with all they have ever been taught? We know they will not change except through the working of the Spirit who can change everything in an instant. We know he can, we know he will someday. The biggest problem, at least for me, is within myself: my lack of patience to wait on his timing, to wait on his sovereign will.*[4]

– 4 –
Church

So far, then, we have seen something of the communication challenge facing some poor cross-cultural missionary.

Happily, it is a challenge that has been overcome in West Africa, many times . . .

A CHURCH IS BORN

On December 15th 1996 a crowd of up to 100,000 people, including the President and Prime Minister of the Sahelian state of Burkina Faso, gathered on a 40-acre site on the outskirts of the capital Ougadougo to give thanks for 75 years of the Assemblies of God denomination in that country.

In that time – in true Assemblies of God style – the AoG in had gone from nothing to being the biggest Protestant denomination with 2,000 congregations and a community of 370,000 adherents aged 12 or above. The church is self-sufficient financially and in this wrenchingly poor country even manages to support, from local sources, such ministries as 'Radio Evangile Developpement', a multi-language, FM radio station.

STIRRING STUFF (I)

The early pioneers, both local and foreign, paid a large price in spiritual heroics to see all this come about. American missionary Eric Booth-Clibborn, for example, died just a few weeks after arriving in Burkina Faso when the work was young. His widow later wrote:

> I call to mind the words written by Eric to his mother shortly before his departure from the United States. 'And now as we turn to Africa, I know how hard it will be for us to part, but our Lord bade us to occupy till He comes, and we are obeying his command without reasoning till our work is done.'
>
> Oh, for more of that implicit trust, that exquisite faith! What a difference it would make for Africa and for every other land if those called responded joyfully, without 'reasoning' or questioning till the work is done.[1]

In 1938, another Assemblies of God missionary couple to the same Mossi people, the Weidmans, lost their six-year-old son to blackwater fever a year after arriving in the country. They themselves suffered illnesses and many other setbacks. All they had left, they decided at one stage, was their faith.

Forty years later they came out of retirement to visit their former home and their nephew recorded what happened:

> An old Mossi pastor, Dokoega, who had watched the Weidmans go through their loss decades earlier, came in from hoeing a field. He was surprised to see Uncle Paul and threw his arms around him. They sang, laughed, and rejoiced together. Then the old pastor said, 'It was not in vain, missionary. There are now churches everywhere!'[2]

STIRRING STUFF (II)

Such stories of expatriates are at least matched by the exploits of the locals.

Take Pastor Koudegma, for example. After training at a Bible school he went back to his home area to start a church. The chief denied him water, but God gave Koudegma a vision of where to dig his own well. He was beaten up by angry mobs, thrown into a well, attacked by a man with a machete.

An observer subsequently came to view the fruits of Koudegma's ministry.

I arrived to find a new church made of mud bricks and palm tree trunks for roof supports. Some 600 people were crowded inside. Koudegma explained, 'This is not the only church. About 10 miles on the other side of the hill is another church of 600 people.'

Koudegma pointed to a group of about 40 people sitting in one area of the church. 'Every one of those people was once demon possessed,' he said, 'and they were brought here for prayer. Sometimes I had to pray for weeks at a time, but now every one of them has been delivered by the power of God.'

Next Koudegma singled out a woman near the front. 'That lady was once a cripple,' he said. 'Now she can walk as well as anyone – healed by the power of God.' Then he pointed to a man near the front. 'He was once blind; now he can see.'

A distinguished man in a long blue robe with white tassels was looking at me. I noticed him and Koudegma caught my look.

'Oh, yes,' he said. 'That is the man who tried to kill me with his machete. When I came back to this town, I found him. I told him there was nothing he could do to kill the love that God had for him. "Even if you kill me, I must tell you that Jesus died for your sins and He wants you to repent and go to heaven," I said.'

Koudegma had a shy grin, and now he showed it. 'The man could not stand the conviction of the Spirit. He fell on his face before God and asked pardon for his sins. God changed him completely. He became a faithful member of this church.'[3]

FAMILIAR STORY

You can find many stories like this, especially in the southern, wetter, greener strips of West Africa. The gospel has been introduced into hundreds of these cultures over the past 200 years and produced a harvest.

WHERE NEXT?

So we can see:

1 Communicating the gospel across cultures is very difficult

But:

2 The gospel has lost none of its ancient, world-turning power, and many peoples of West Africa have proven this for themselves.

> *In the last days*
> *the mountain of the Lord's temple will be established*
> *as chief among the mountains,*
> *it will be raised above the hills,*
> *and all nations will stream to it.*
>
> *Many peoples will come and say,*
> *'Come, let us go up to the mountain of the Lord,*
> *to the house of the God of Jacob.*
> *He will teach us his ways,*
> *so that we may walk in his paths.'[4]*

Next we ask, What is the picture across all of West Africa? How developed is this Christian movement? Where is it small or non-existent? And what (as this series of books tries to ask) remains as the pioneer task for Christ's church?

GREAT NIGERIA

Nigeria spells out the West African story in extra-large letters. This country is to West Africa what a tabloid newspaper headline is to the news itself: lurid, overstated, but a good place to start. Nigeria's population (100m or so, nobody knows), its political problems, religious ferment, the stories of sin and grace: all are on an epic scale.

Nigeria is large enough to encompass every different West African strip. You find a southern region of Christian/animist farmers, a northern region of Muslim/animist cattle herders, and a mixed, troubled, and changing zone in the middle.[5]

THE SOUTH

In the south, you find the Church is long-established:

- Millions of people have turned to Christ and are sincerely following him. Nigeria is a spiritual super-power. Its church outshines that of any western nation with the possible exception of that of the United States. The Church of England in Nigeria, for example, contains many more worshippers than the Church of England in England; arguably the Anglican communion ought to consider a name-change ('the Nigerian communion', perhaps).

- Charismatics and evangelicals have become a massive force among the Nigerian middle classes. A renewal began in the 1970s and spread through the universities. According to one Nigerian scholar 'charismatic Christians are the most dynamic element in Nigerian Christianity, affecting millions of educated young people.'[6]

As well as working in evangelism, Nigerian believers are healing the sick, casting out demons, praying hard, cooperating in social action to 'heal the nation', becoming conscientiously involved in Nigeria's nightmarish politics, attacking poverty, and sending missionaries and teachers out around the world.

This is, at best, a holistic, African, full-blooded Christianity, attempting to apply Christ's salvation to all of life.

- Entangled in with all this, though, are the 'spiritual' churches and Christians. These are the people who mix Christianity with Traditional Religion.

The activity of the spirituals is, of course, exactly what you would expect given the mind-set we talked about in Chapter Two: some people want spiritual power wherever they can find it. If 'Christ' offers a special magic they are willing to add him to their pantheon. But they not willing to serve 'Christ alone' and as such must make God despair. They may be formally

> *Those who cling to worthless idols*
> *Forfeit the grace that could be theirs*[7]

numbered as part of Nigeria's Christian community but in fact they have far more in common with the Old Testament people of Israel during a bad patch.

One survey of a small Local Government Area in Lagos State – one of the first parts of West Africa ever to encounter the gospel – suggested as many as 70% of the 'Christian' community were actually 'spirituals'. The survey concluded: 'the region which served as the main entrance for the gospel into Nigeria is decaying spiritually before us.'[8]

- The Church, even in the Christianized places, still has many needs – especially for theological lecturers, and for people prepared to care for churches outside the villages and towns.

THE NORTH

Meanwhile the north is another world. Run by the Fulbe and Hausa, chirruping with the incantations of the folk Islam practitioners, northern Nigeria is a spiritual jungle of folk Islamic practices. Christian presence is small and scattered and folk Islam largely goes unchallenged. Here are a few examples from the strange twilight world that is the 'northern' type peoples (from a recent survey):

- 30,000 Boko. 'Some time ago ECWA missionaries won some Boko to Christ at Kigbura. Some backslid due to threats and persecution. Only 5 remained Christians. Then, one of the missionaries died as a result of alleged bewitching, and Kigbura was left without a worker.[9]

- 100,000 Bolewa. 'There is a big baobab tree at Daniski. It is said that at certain times the tree lies flat on the ground though usually it stays upright. A festival is connected with this tree and a yearly sacrifice is performed at its base. School children and other people make excursions to Daniski to see the tree.

  'The Bolewa do all they can to propagate Islam. They are proud that they are one of the first Muslim tribes in Nigeria, and that they are all Muslims and no Bole is Christian.'[10]

- 100,000 Ganagana. Ganagana land offers 'an oracle called Kajigi which is consulted even by important personalities around Nigeria. It is said that Kajigi can tell anybody anything in the world if the person approaches it.[11]

- 20,000 Kutin, enslaved and converted to Islam in the Fulbe Jihad. They still retain elements of their traditional religion (headquartered in Cameroon.) 'Nunvore is the god [or jinn] of thunder who has made the Kutin people famous among their neighbouring tribes. The thunder kills anyone who steals anything. It is very effective. Yikangerum is a women's cult. Any man who disobeys the orders of this cult is paralyzed immediately, until he repents and offers sacrifices and beer.'[12]

THE MIDDLE

In the middle of Nigeria you find a great spiritual commotion. Surely something is happening and that thing is the turning of people from Muslim and Traditional Religion backgrounds to Christ.

Yet beyond that bare statement it is hard to know the truth. Statistics are unreliable. Rumours fly around and you can find all kinds of amazing stories of mass conversions to Christ. I've been told by a Nigerian Christian leader, for example, that the sight of former Imams preaching Christ on the streets is 'very very common.' Both the Muslims and the Christians in Nigeria believe these stories.

There have been riots, murders and church-burnings on the basis of these perceived truths. As many as 6000 Christians have been killed in religious riots within the 1990s. In July 1995, for example, rioting by local Muslims in Tafawa Belewa Local Government Area of Bauchi State in Central Nigeria destroyed more than 70 churches. During one church service, 31 Christians were killed.[13]

Unfortunately (and here are the mind-set issues again) African worldviews are such that wild and improbable stories are readily believed and passed on. Many of them are certainly not true.

At the same time, some of them certainly *are* true. Any honest student of the Bible or church history will have to admit that wild and improbable things actually do happen. It is our Western mindset that tries to persuade us they cannot. Millions of people have turned to Christ in Nigeria in the past few decades and that movement certainly continues today. Under the dust and confusion that is central Nigeria, God's kingdom is advancing. Beyond that, we can't say.

A FIRST LOOK

Our brief look at Nigeria gives us clues as to what we will see across West Africa: some places are long-established with Christian witness, though with problems of their own; some are in rapid transition; and many places are hardly touched. God is at work, and as you might perhaps expect, everywhere, it's a mess.

– 5 –
Pioneers

A REGULAR PATTERN

Larry Vanderaa, an American missionary who for more than a decade has spent many months each year living in the simplest fashion in a Fulbe village in Mali, has compiled the most authoritative surveys of mission activity and church growth in francophone West Africa.

According to Vanderaa, the progress of the gospel in each one of West Africa's peoples falls into one of four broad stages.

- Stage 1: Missionaries arrive and begin to bear witness. Then, for a missionary lifetime or so, 20–40 years, nothing happens. Perhaps you may find a handful of converts by the end. But all through this time, Vanderaa suggests, 'the Gospel is slowly penetrating the hearts and minds of the people.'[1]

- Stage 2: 'The church begins to grow slowly until the Christians comprise about 3–5% of the ethnic group.' This is the stage when national Christians are most feeling the heat from the rest of their people, where local Christian pioneers are slowly, and often at great cost, establishing an authentic Christian life and community within their culture, for the very first time.

- Stage 3 is that part you read about in Christian magazines. 'The church enters a period of explosive growth as the Gospel takes root in the society as a whole and the number of Christians may increase from 5% to 20%-40% of the ethnic group in 10–20 years.'[2] This is an era of miracles, big evangelistic rallies, mass conversions to Christ, great church planting movements. The Mossi church in Burkina Faso, its foundations laid at such cost, is in this group; so are churches among some peoples in Central Nigeria, as well as Chad, Côte d'Ivoire, Senegal and Togo.

- Stage 4 is the stage familiar to us all in the West, as being most like home. 'Growth begins to slow or even stops altogether. If the church has not been

well taught in stages 2 and 3, nominalism creeps in followed by years (then centuries?) of recurrent cycles of backsliding and revival.'[3] The pioneer task is over; the people are not necessarily individually Christians – far from it – but they can't say they have nowhere to go, or no examples to follow, or no community to join, where they will not see the Christian faith lived out among their own people.

Vanderaa backs up his thesis with maps showing the different times missionaries first started working in a culture, compared with the current state of the Christian church, and it's impressive stuff.

Where the missionaries entered prior to 1920, you can now see large Christian communities (and also many problems with spiritualism).

Peoples where missions entered more recently have Christian movements that are at earlier stages of development, some seeing large-scale turnings to Christ, some seeing local people living out the Christian life for the first time, some seeing almost nothing at all.

And Vanderaa's analysis holds essentially true over all sorts of denominations, mission organizations and strategies – which is depressing news to those who think they uniquely have an inside track on the Holy Spirit's power. Some missiologies are indeed more effective than others. But on the whole, God does not appear to have favourites.

ONLY NOW

Vanderaa's work offers a neat explanation for West Africa's spiritual patchwork. The gospel-less peoples are, simply, the ones that Christ's Church has not effectively tackled yet. We don't see churches all across the Sahel because:

1 It takes time and

2 Only now, after twenty centuries, is a comprehensive mission effort being organized.

The big obstacle to Sahelian peoples responding to the gospel is the old and obvious one. No-one's gone and told them the Good News. Or, to be slightly more fair, the people who have gone have not in general yet stayed long enough for their hard work to bear fruit.

This rule has, of course, brilliant exceptions. One American couple, the Watkins, did pioneering work among the Fulbe in Guinea for over forty years, starting in 1923. They did not see a harvest, but now, Fulbe who were influenced by this dogged and much-loved missionary family are turning to Christ.

In most of the Northern Sahel, however, the initial work started only between the mid-1970s and the present day, as part of the current intensification of frontier mission activity around the world.[4] More missions started work among more Sahelian peoples during the 1980s than in the whole period between 1945 through to 1979 and, possibly, than in the whole period from AD 30 through to 1979.

<table>
<tr><td>

LEARNING FULFULDE, THE LANGUAGE OF THE FULBE

Our facial muscles need limbering up, and our tongues lubricated before each lesson; sucking a lemon is helpful.[5]

</td><td>

So right now, all across the Sahel, missions are struggling with the slow, unglamorous, very early stages of teaching Christ within a culture. There are many signs that their work is bearing fruit – every major Sahelian people has some small number of Christians among them now, a dozen here, sixty there – but there is also every sign that years of patient witness lie ahead.

</td></tr>
</table>

Sahelian missionaries feel isolated and scattered, they battle with climate and cross-cultural misunderstanding and they have little to encourage them, beyond the lessons of history and the promises of God.

SAHELIAN PEOPLES

Who are these Sahelian pioneer peoples? Anthropologists sometimes teach about 'Great Tradition' cultures, cultures that set the agenda, and 'Little Tradition' cultures, cultures that follow the agenda set by others. You can find both types in the Sahel, and neither has had their fair share of Christian witness. The lack of a Great Tradition Christian Sahelian culture is one reason why the gospel has not yet commended itself to the Sahel.

GREAT TRADITIONS

All the peoples of West Africa's former empires – many, like the Fulbe and Wolof embodying 'great traditions' within Islam – are in the unreached category.

The Fulbe are the largest nomadic people in the world, with a population of between 18m and 25m, depending on how many settled groups you also include. They are West Africa's cattle herders (supplying 90% of Nigeria's beef for

example) and are found throughout the region. They started becoming Muslims in the 11th century and are proud to have led the Islamization campaigns in the 19th century.

Fulbe are not wimps. They are trained from birth to be tough, brave, reserved, dignified, modest, treating even their enemies with chivalry and respect; and hospitable: 'your guest is your god' is a typical proverb.

Larry Vanderaa describes his Fulbe friends like this:

They are the Fulbe, the conquerors of the Sahel, conquering both its physical hardships and its peoples. They are the descendants of the proud, fearless warriors that rode out over the Sahel in the past centuries conquering all of the Sahel from Dakar to Kano in the name of Islam. They are the great missionaries of Islam, the aristocrats of the Sahel. They submit to no-one but Allah.[6]

> *In the Sahel, one missionary wearily told me, 'there are very many Muslims, and very few missionaries.'*

The Fulbe are probably the largest of West Africa's unreached peoples. Others – looking roughly from west to east – include:

- The Wolof of Senegal and Gambia, 3m people among whom there are, at a generous estimate, 50 Christians. Senegambian Islam is a unique variant of Islam within West Africa. It is dominated by two large brotherhoods. The brotherhoods run local pilgrimage sites, fix up jobs, provide hospitality, run youth centres, advise the government and generally act as a sort of spiritual trades union for Senegambian men. Marabouts, who are a kind of middle management in the brotherhood system, have a great influence over people's lives, as personal counsellors, as spiritual power brokers and even, sometimes, as saviours from sin. For a number of Senegalese, the marabout's word is what they are trusting to get them into heaven.

- The Tuareg: nomadic peoples of the desert, respected even by the Fulbe. The Tuaregs have had an unhappy recent history: their homeland carved up between Mali and Niger, they have been on the losing side in all kinds of civil conflict and droughts. There are a handful of little Tuareg Christian congregations around the region. Tuareg jewellery often uses the sign of the cross, a pointer understood by some to a Tuareg pre-Christian past.

- The Maures: another people of the desert, who live mostly in Mauretania. Legal restrictions to Christian work in Mauretania, and the harsh environment and poverty there, mean Maures are especially remote and isolated from the gospel.

- The Bambara (3m plus) are the dominant tribe of Mali, most of them Muslim farmers. Fifteen percent or so of this people never submitted to Islam and from this group a church is slowly emerging. Related to the Bambara are other unreached Muslim groups, notably the radically-Islamic tradesmen, the Jula. Guinea's strongly Muslim Maninka people are also relatives.

- The Songhai, further east from the Bambara, had their turn at empire back in the 12th century and have shown little response to the gospel; in Mali there were only around 60 Christians out of a population of 600,000 at the last count.

- The Hausa, who along with the Fulbe dominate the politics of Nigeria, are another great Muslim people, though with also a good deal of response to Christ.[7]

- The 4.5m Kanuri of north-eastern Nigeria and the Lake Chad region. By tradition said to come from Yemen, they grew by conquering and assimilating small tribes around them and presided over a thousand-year-long Muslim kingdom. Possibly fewer than 20 converts to Christ were identified from among them in Nigeria at the last count.[8]

GREAT COMPLEXITY

Open the lid on these large peoples and you find yet more layers of subtlety and complexity – as you would expect.

Take the Wodaabe, for example. These 100,000 people are Fulbe, but they only marry other Wodaabe, indicating that they were perhaps a separate tribe who somewhere in history merged with the Fulbe. Nomads who range far across their homelands in Niger and elsewhere, Wodaabe are among the least-Islamized of the Fulbe. They are famous for their magic spells and amulets: in their portfolio is magic to make themselves almost irresistible to women. (Or so they say.)

This unlikely sounding group of people (their name means 'people to avoid') are, among the first of all the Fulbe family to respond to Christ. Missions like World Horizons, the Southern Baptists, and particularly SIM have seen Wodaabe turn to Christ in some numbers.

Or take the Manga, a 100,000-strong subgroup of the Kanuri people, living on the edge of the Sahara. SIM has been working among them for over 30 years, Bible translation and literacy work are ongoing (thanks to the agency SIL), but still hardly a Christian is known among them.

CASE STUDY: AMONG THE WODAABE

One of the SIM missionaries who was in at the birth and early years of the Wodaabe church, wrote about the challenge of doing authentic Christian ministry among 'the people to avoid':

Imagine you're the missionary, giving grain to starving herdsmen. Right now how do you know that your action isn't just buying their allegiance to Christ?

Or try this - how would you disciple a dozen groups of believers within a radius of hundreds of kilometers in the bush, where there are few roads and where your intended audience has often moved on without trace by the time you reach their camp?

How do you administer a development programme 200 kilometers away via unbelievably rough roads?

And how do you ask folk to be self-sufficient and experiment with alien farming practices in a country where it hardly ever rains?

How do you patiently sit by without interfering or trying to push them too fast while the fragile, embryonic Christian Fulani community works through the issues of polygamy and church leadership?[9]

Or another example: travelling alongside the Tuareg, and sometimes counted as part of them, are the Inaden people. They are blacksmiths, jewellers, leathermakers, and wood- and stone-carvers for the Tuareg. Considered by the Tuareg to be socially inferior, they are feared for their black magic, called upon for their midwifery skills, and exist alongside the Tuareg as a symbiotic but separate people. No Christian witness among them is known.

LITTLE TRADITIONS

On the edges of the desert you can also locate hundreds of small villages and communities, remote and poor. Linguistic and cultural differences among them mean that ethnographers look upon them all as separate peoples, even though the total population of each is only that of a small town or a village elsewhere.

While many of the men in these peoples are multilingual, and so not entirely cut off from opportunities to encounter the Good News, many of the women and children are not. Poor, female, isolated by geography and culture: here indeed is remoteness from the gospel.

– 6 –
Time and patience

We have seen that the churches and missions are in the very early stages of preaching Christ within the remaining unreached peoples of the Sahel. In this chapter we look at some of the players in this drama.

Among them are:

- Local people
- Foreign missionaries
- Pray-ers
- Development workers

LOCAL PEOPLE

Local people are meeting Jesus and forming characters, lifestyles and communities that reflect him. Even among the hardest peoples and those most neglected by the Church you can find the stirring of a response.

Alhaji, for example, was a tailor from a group of Fulbe who had settled long ago in Guinea. To make some money, he moved his shop to The Gambia. While he was there, one of his customers gave him a Christian book.

After years of reading and struggle, Alhaji turned to Christ, being (so far as he thought) the first of the Fulbe to do so: 'I could believe,' he later wrote, 'that all my sins were forgiven now and that I could start a new life, almost like a baby, without any record of bad deeds. A deep joy filled me.'

But going against the grain of his traditions was every bit as hard as he expected. His wife left him. His father told him to return to Islam and take a second wife. When Alhaji refused, his father started to beat him and strangle him; only the arrival of the police saved Alhaji's life.

Later, after Alhaji was reconciled with both his wife and his father, God called him to return to his home village in Guinea. Alhaji was risking his life, the chief refused to protect him, but a number of people accepted his message, not least after the Christians prayed for the daughter of a local spiritual practitioner and saw her miraculously healed.

The church struggled into life, a tiny Christian witness among millions of Islamic Fulbe. Several times people threatened to burn down his home, which served as the church building. One Sunday, the Christians gathered early, having been specifically warned that the church would be torched that day. All through the morning they sang and rejoiced and nothing happened. Around lunchtime they found that the Imam who had ordered the burning had died in the night.

And these are only the headline-grabbing struggles. Deeper than these are the slower ones: the fight to construct on previously unploughed soil Christian life, Christian rituals, and a Christian community, and to ensure that all of them are authentically Fulbe as well as truly Christian – and all this just to bring the gospel to birth in one Fulbe town.

BREATHTAKING

It's fashionable in our context to illustrate the flaws in all these partly-finished projects. But some of what God is doing among these peoples who are meeting Christ for the first time is deeply impressive.

You find Christians opening their homes not just for an evening but for months to people who have been cut off from their own families because of their faith. You find depths of worship and of Christian life. A story from a people in Burkina Faso among whom there is currently a rapid turning to Christ:

We had a day of prayer and fasting one day recently at church . . . for rain as it had been weeks since the last rain and the meningitis epidemic is still ravaging [the town]. Praise the Lord the rain has at last come making it very humid.

The people are happy as this should stop the meningitis. We have lost a number of children from the church. In one family in which the parents have only known the Lord for a year, they lost five of their seven children in less than four months (two in one day). Just a couple of weeks ago we buried the second child in one family to die within twelve days. The father stood up in the worship part of the service last Sunday and really lifted us all up in worship. Don't think it hasn't been hard for these families. It is but they are determined to trust the Lord.[1]

MISSIONARIES

The missionaries that arrived among the frontier peoples of the Sahel in the 1970s, 1980s and 1990s come in all colours, and from all continents: some from elsewhere in Africa, others from new centres like Brazil and Korea, still others from Western countries.

All of them are choosing the unglamorous end of the line in Christian ministry. Bright young workers disappear into the sands for a couple of decades, returning home mottled by the sun and out of touch, and with almost nothing to show for their years away.

It's a tough, unhealthy, lonely environment. One missionary told me, 'We spent the first couple of years here hoping we'd get some nasty disease so that we could return home with honour.'

They may feel they hardly ever seem to share the gospel in words, a frustrating experience for the zealous evangelicals who make up the missionary force. Many simply show love to all-comers in whatever ways open to them: running or organizing clinics; teaching in schools; working on various small-scale relief projects such as planting acacia trees or running an 'animal bank' for nomads who lost their wealth in a famine.

Yet unconditional love is surely the right 'strategy'. One YWAM missionary described their work as 'weaving a web of justice, love, righteousness, compassion.'[3]

It's always slow. Some tell the whole story of the Bible slowly over a couple of years, leaving time for discussion and interaction. Others work on Bible translation.

Incarnation is a vital principle: living with the people, borrowing things off them, laughing and crying with them, staying with them through all their trials.

Larry Vanderaa, a self-confessed 'strategy nut', attempts to be a 'Jesus Marabout' in his adopted home village. As a way of getting quick results, it is about as effective as farming giant tortoises – but it is a strategy rich with love and integrity:

> I certainly could not be a very impressive Marabou [he wrote]. We were like babes in the woods. We had to be shown everything. And they taught us how to live in that harsh context – in the Fulbe way. They fixed up our huts with beautiful Fulbe mats – the Fulbe way. They showed us how to make tea – the Fulbe way. They showed us what to wear and what to eat. They taught us how to speak Fulfulde – according to them the real Fulbe Fulfulde. I tried to milk and herd cattle, Ann tried to weave mats, the children became involved with their friends. We attended naming ceremonies, weddings and funerals. We bought cattle and oxen and a plow and made our own millet field. We tried as much as we could to become part of the Fulbe life.[4]

All of this deadly slow and humble activity, 'the plod of God', seems to be the only authentic way to bring the gospel with integrity across the cultural chasms.

Vanderaa again:

> For whatever reason, it appears that the Spirit, at least for now, is building the church among the Fulbe in a manner consistent with the history of mission work in Africa: deliberately, laying the foundation brick by brick over time. Thus in Fulbe evangelism, by and large we are in the first 25 years. Work among the Fulbe is not for the faint-hearted, the easily discouraged. We must not weary in well-doing.

THE PRAY-ERS

Working in quite another sphere are those who serve in prayer.

To the non-missions specialist, it's something of a surprise to find mailing lists and internet conferences for people around the world who are committed to serving Sahelian peoples in prayer.

Some mission agencies (YWAM for example) have staff devoted full-time to marshalling prayer for the Sahel, gathering information and organizing prayer tours for overseas visitors.

Other people get involved in their spare time, seeing in their intercession some contribution to the welfare of these far-away peoples:

> To loose the chains of injustice
>   and untie the cords of the yoke
> To set the oppressed free
>   and break every yoke[5]

John Bardsley, a home-based WEC missionary, describes how he became a prayer advocate for the Jola people of Senegal.[6]

It started very simply – a letter from Senegal made me seriously angry.

'The Jola people have had a church for 30 years, but it is not growing because there is hardly a Christian who is totally free from traditional occult practices.'

I was angry with the devil for binding these people. I was also angry with myself and with the mission's prayer force. Our prayers had not been sufficient for God to empower the missionaries and set the Jola free.

The Lord would not let me rest. In 1986 I began to spend one lunch hour each week in intercession for the Jolas.

Others joined him. He sent out a monthly letter containing news from all the missionaries who worked among the Jola. He dug out a secular anthropology paper on the Jola, which, among other things, taught him about their traditional shrines and gods. He organized a prayer trek to Senegal, listening to and praying for church leaders and missionaries.

For me, prayer warfare has been a great stimulus to holiness – my intercession is powerless unless I am clean! It is the best thing that has happened to me for 20 years!

After ten years of this spare-time ministry, he was able to do an evaluation:

When one missionary retired in 1988 after 33 years among the Jola people, she wondered if her whole life's work had been in vain. Even in 1990, when she went back for a visit, she saw little to encourage her. However, when she came on the prayer trek in 1996, she could see the difference!

The situation was vastly changed from that of ten years before:

One church is now thriving with over 80 people. They are free from the fear of spirits and are discipling 40 new converts, mainly high-school students. They plan to plant three more churches in the villages these students come from.

Another two churches are growing, with an attendance of at least 30, and there are fledgling churches and evangelistic Bible study groups in other centres. In addition, 64 Jola believers attend multi-ethnic churches, and there are several individual Christians in non-Christian villages.

Six pastors are already qualified and serving in their churches, while others are in training.

The breakthrough has begun – in answer to prayer. Of course, this is not only due to the intercession of the Jola prayer team. Our prayers have been added to those of two generations of missionaries and their supporters, but we know we are making a valuable contribution, and current missionaries have become grateful friends.

Emmanuel Olewa, leader of the Senegal team of the Nigerian mission agency Capro, has made a study of the occult forces in charge of Senegal, according to the perceptions of the Traditional Religion practitioners. He uses this information in his own prayers. He told me, 'I believe the Lord wants to thoroughly, thoroughly reveal the enemy [Satan and the occult spirits] so that he can be thoroughly, thoroughly overcome.'

Of his own adopted home town in Senegal, he says:

> It is easy to know now that the whole city has been covenanted with the powers of darkness. This ruling spirit has a ruling covenant with the whole city . . . This is something that is clear. Everybody knows.

Armed with his research and open to the leading of the Holy Spirit, he and his team have specifically sought to destroy through prayer every evil foundation, covenant, or agreement that the local people may have made with evil spirits. And they are seeking to see their city established on righteous foundations. Other people have also been using the information to pray.

Since they began praying along those lines, a church that has been established for the first time in his town, after many years of unsuccessful attempts. Local people are turning to Christ in increasing numbers (he has measured this) and finding grace to stand in the midst of persecution. Some are working as full-time Christian workers: all this is new, and it all post-dates the prayer campaigns.[7]

DEVELOPMENT WORKERS

Development is the necessary attempt to rebalance the scales of social justice in the Sahel, and so is also certainly an area in which God is at work. But God does not have this field to himself. Development is a multinational industry, which itself is captive to the world of politics.

It is beyond the scope of this book to figure out a coherent way of showing practical compassion to our fellow human beings through development aid. So much is counter-productive. But we can make the following points:

- Much of the money spent is shockingly wasted and harms the communities it intends to help. The invisible cultural barriers are too high a hurdle for many a scheme. Well-meaning amateurs, Christians included, and well-equipped governments both stumble. Millions have been spent equipping West Africa with what are now broken tractors, empty shells of clinic buildings, or fridges intended for child-vaccines that have mysteriously been ghosted away to urban pizza restaurants. You have probably funded some of this: I'm sure I have.

One not especially cynical source told me that the most good that some Non-Governmental Organizations do is that they set up an office, hire chauffeurs, secretaries, guards, gardeners and thus contribute to the local economy. Otherwise, West Africa would be better off without them.

- A lot of good work, however, is being done through both Christian and non-Christian agencies, work that enhances people's lives, work that has the flavour of God's kingdom about it.

> Marks of a successful development project, as worked out by a gathering of evangelical Christian relief agencies:
>
> - Long-term (or at least part of long-term relationship)
> - Suggested, owned and in part resourced by local people
> - Respecting local knowledge
> - On which off-the-spot authorities (like local political leaders or foreign donors) don't prescribe what should be done
> - Cares about the integrity of process more than a specific outcome.[8]

One evangelical development agency considers the most effective initiatives are those that mobilize the local community through a committed Christian facilitator. Another respected Christian development expert comments that the only truly sustainable development is 'developing people'. A third told me she now only worked on projects that local people themselves dreamed up.

- Development money is not, in the final analysis, what the Sahel is really short of. Christian character is. The agency Tear Fund, interestingly, prefers to talk of 'transformation' rather than 'development', attempting to reflect this reality. We need to be wary of anyone who asks us to fund a 'quick fix': the money squandered on development in West Africa at least has proved there's no such thing.

– 7 –
Future

What does the future hold?

TO THE CITIES

A deep and painful current of change is flowing through the Sahel's cultures.

The young people, especially the men, are abandoning the hardships of village life for the hope of a modern, better life in the cities.

Education is playing a part in this: once someone has got schooling they don't usually want to go back to growing millet and weaving baskets. Inter-ethnic conflict, and the changing shape of the Sahara are two other factors sending people to the cities.

Some of these young men disappear completely so far as their extended families are concerned. Others leave a wife and family in the village, coming home in the rainy season to father another child (and perhaps unwittingly spread West Africa's own distinctive variant of HIV). Still others take their wives but leave their parents.

All this is eating away at ancient cultural patterns. The extended family is the bedrock of African social structure and, said one African commentator, it 'has crumpled under the pressure of social, cultural, political and economic changes in Africa.'[1]

Communities are breaking up: elders, wives, and children are scratching a living in the villages; the young men or small families are making a home in the cities. Older people grieve that the younger ones are losing everything that made them decent and noble. For the peoples of the Sahel, this period has a turbulent, end-of-an-era feel.

This is a great call on the Church:

1 We can affirm that it is not wrong to move to the cities. Urbanization is not necessarily a 'bad thing'. Many people are forced to the cities by misfortune; but plenty come because they want to, because they are fed up of village life or of leading their flocks around Africa. Or they come because it is the only way they know to improve their economic health.

   Cities embody a hope of a better life. And Christians affirm that it is good for individuals and peoples to seek to improve their lot so long as it is consistent with loving others and loving God. The Bible itself starts with the human species in the bush but ends with redeemed human beings in a city. No cultures are static: sometimes it is right to change. We can affirm the aspirations that take people to the cities.

2 The Church can also demonstrate that urban life does not have to be less principled or less honourable than the traditions forged for survival through many generations of rural Sahelian life. Through Christ, moral values can outlast cultural changes; indeed Christ builds lives new and better.

The Church has a call to support peoples and cultures when they are being shaken and broken, and to demonstrate how faith in Christ can help them through the changes.

AN OPPORTUNE TIME

Urbanization also offers a wonderful opportunity for the Church to pay off some of its debts, to bring the news of Christ's love to even the remotest peoples.

As we know from the West African worldview, the great need for a young person entering a city is a network of contacts, an extended family, a support and social security system.

Thousands of young people have become Muslims in the cities because Islam offers that kind of ready-made community. In Côte d'Ivoire perhaps half of the four million or so recent entrants to Abidjan have become Muslim, even though in the country as a whole the Church is growing much faster than is Islam.

People will enter Christian communities for the same reason. There are dangers here, particularly that people enter Christianity simply as an attempt to adapt to urban life. Here is one of the ways 'spiritual' Christians arise. But assuming the faith can be taught well enough to reach the heart, it's an exciting time.

- Peoples from remote villages are being gathered together and are themselves learning languages in which they may hear the gospel.

- The barriers of tradition and culture are certainly lower in the cities than the villages. You can talk openly about Christ here in ways impossible in many Muslim villages.

- People are more willing to change, having already made the great transition of leaving behind their rural lives.

- Cities make possible urban, trade-language churches in which young people from many different Sahelian cultures can find a home.

- The church worldwide, especially its evangelical wing, has historically grown strongly in newly industrializing countries. It still is today. That also may point to great hope for West Africa's cities.

IN THE SAHEL

Growing cities feature large in the future, and missionaries are surely right to locate themselves in these strategic places. But the Church will always have debts to the countryside of the Sahel. Here are a couple of reasons – one tactical, one to do with love, integrity and the nature of God.

- *Tactics*: Despite the urbanizing trend, most of the Sahel's peoples still live in rural communities. It's wrong to neglect them. In Senegal, for example, three-quarters of the population are rural. Most of them have no church and little contact with Christians.

- *The call of love*: The Church dishonours Christ if its only message to rural peoples like Fulbe nomadic pastoralists is 'settle down in the cities and we'll meet you there.' If we are bringing a gospel that only works for urban

environments, it isn't the gospel. Every culture, like every individual, bears both the Creator's signature and sin's graffiti. Every one can be cleaned up and then fulfilled through Christ.

So Christians have a duty to stand up for these peoples of the Sahel whose cultures are being assaulted by the twin forces of environmental degradation and Westernization. These cultures, as much as any cultures around the world, are expressions of the image of God. Christ can be glorified in them. There can be a redeemed, fulfilled Fulbe nomadic code of ethics, for example, that is far superior even to the one they already proudly own.

Larry Vanderaa:

> *The Fulbe will reject any new system or religion that would require them to deny their heritage or their identity or significantly alter their culture. It is imperative that their culture and their identity be affirmed in Jesus' name. Only as this is done will the Fulbe consider belief in Jesus a viable option. Fulbe culture is not perfect, there will have to be some transformation, but it can be affirmed, it can be redeemed.*[2]

It will surely happen some day – when communities of Christian Fulbe live out a nomadic pastoral lifestyle to the glory of God. It will happen through time, patience, and the faithful obedience of Christians to Christ's commands. It may even happen as part of the wave of mission effort and prayer that has swelled across the region since the mid-1970s.

But it has not happened yet.

NOTES

CHAPTER 1

1 Chris Brazier in *New Internationalist*, June 1995, p 24.

2 United Nations Development Index, 1993.

3 Isaiah 58:10–11.

4 *Operation World* figures 1993.

5 *Islam Shall Hear* (2/1996), Red Sea Mission Team.

6 Infant mortality rates for the mid-1990s were 4.7 per thousand for Singapore and an estimated 110 per thousand for Mali.

7 'In AD 210 Libyan-born Septimus Severus, Emperor of Rome, arrived to inspect Hadrian's wall where a unit of Ethiopians were stationed at Abbalava (now Burgh-by-Sands) near Carlisle.' (The *Observer* (London) 20th Jan 1996, p 16, quoting *Africans in Britain before 1560*, P Edwards, 1981.)

8 Micah 6:8.

CHAPTER 2

1 Fairy tales, of course, have their origin in days when this kind of outlook on the world was prominent in our own societies.

2 *Alhaji's Journey to Life*, privately published by WEC Gambia, p 10.

3 *Alhaji's Journey to Life*, privately published by WEC Gambia, p 8,9.

4 I'm grateful to David Maranz for this analysis.

5 [Paul G Hiebert and Eloise Hiebert Meneses, *Incarnational Ministry* 1995, Baker Books, p 196: 'In peasant societies [and tribal ones] people focus their attention on subsistence and on maintaining relationships. Economic concerns are subordinate to social obligations to the family, caste, and community and to religious obligations to the ancestors, spirits, and gods.' P 199: 'The result is that the peasant household is not controlled primarily by economic values such as productivity or profit, but by social and religious values that emphasize the importance of maintaining relationships with people, ancestors, spirits and gods.'

CHAPTER 3

1 That is, belonging to the Fulbe people: Pullo is the singular, Fulbe the plural.

2 Ancestor worship ought to be a problem. It is central to African Traditional Religion but forbidden in Islam. In practice, however, ancestor worship occurs throughout the Islamic world.

3 The full version of this story appeared in the Gambia *Daily Observer*, September 1st 1994, under the headline 'The Battle for Bia's Soul.'

4 Larry Vanderaa, in a paper presented to an internal WEC conference on the Fulbe in Banjul, The Gambia, September 1997.

CHAPTER 4

1 George O Wood in *Mountain Movers*, (Assemblies of God Division of Foreign Missions) June 1997, p 6–7.

2 George O Wood in *Mountain Movers*, (Assemblies of God Division of Foreign Missions) June 1997, p 7.

3 *Mountain Movers*, (Assemblies of God Division of Foreign Missions) June 1997, p 17.

4 Isaiah 2:2-3 and Micah 4:1-2.

5 It's not entirely accurate because Nigeria's peoples are rather mingled together so you will find, for example, churches full of southerners in the northern regions.

6 Matthews A Ojo, *International Bulletin of Missionary Research*, July 1995, p 114.

7 Jonah 2:8.

8 Niyi Gbade, report on Badagry Local Government Area in Lagos State, AD2000 Movement Nigeria, 1996, p 8.

9 *Priority Focus: Some Unreached People Groups in Nigeria*, AD 2000 Nigeria Movement 1996, p 9.

10 *Priority Focus: Some Unreached People Groups in Nigeria*, AD 2000 Nigeria Movement 1996, p 10.

11 *Priority Focus: Some Unreached People Groups in Nigeria*, AD 2000 Nigeria Movement 1996, p 23.

12 *Priority Focus: Some Unreached People Groups in Nigeria*, AD 2000 Nigeria Movement 1996, p 42.

13 Open Doors *Newsbrief* 5/96, p 3.

CHAPTER 5

1 Larry Vanderaa, *A Survey for Christian Reformed World Missions of Missions and Churches in West Africa*, May 1991, p 116. Copies of this survey are available from Christian Reformed World Missions, 2850 Kalamazoo SE, Grand Rapids, MI 49560, USA. Fax 1 616-246-0834.

2 Larry Vanderaa, *A Survey for Christian Reformed World Missions of Missions and Churches in West Africa*, May 1991, p 116.

3 Larry Vanderaa, *A Survey for Christian Reformed World Missions of Missions and Churches in West Africa*, May 1991, p 117.

4 Other earlier pioneers include WEC among the Fulbe in the 1930s, SIM in southern Niger since the 1940s, and the Evangelical Baptists in Timbuktu and Gao among the Songhai and Tuareg peoples since 1953.

5 Phil & Marion Grasham, learning Fulfulde in Mali, quoted March 1998.

6 In a paper presented to an internal WEC conference on the Fulbe in Banjul, The Gambia, September 1997.

7 *Operation World* reports that the turning to Christ is concentrated among a section of the Hausa known as the Maguzawa, who are the least Islamic of the Hausa.
Many people use the Hausa language even though they are not themselves ethnically Hausa: this explains the many Hausa-speaking congregations you find all across the Nigeria.

8 *Priority Focus: Some Unreached People Groups in Nigeria*, AD 2000 Nigeria Movement 1996 p 35.

9 Mark Burt in SIM UK *View*, Winter 1993 'What's the right thing to do?'

CHAPTER 6

1 Eileen Summerville of WEC in a private newsletter, June 1997.

2 A pastor among the Fulbe people, 1997.

3 Jean-Marc Fritsch in a personal interview in Dakar, Senegal, October 1997.
4 Larry Vanderaa, from notes given to a WEC conference on the Fulbe, Banjul, Gambia, September 1997.
5 Isaiah 58:6.
6 This is from the WEC UK magazine *Worldwide*, Jan–Feb 1998, pp 4–5.
7 That does not mean that the prayer campaigns were somehow fruitful and earlier forms of evangelism were not. Scripture teaching is that one person sows, and another reaps (see 1 Corinthians 3:5–15). It is better to see all the different efforts as the steady development of God's sovereign purpose through time.
8 See Ewert, D. Merrill, Peter Clark, and Paul Eberts 1993, *Worldview and sustainable community development* paper presented at the annual conference of the Association of Evangelical Relief and Development Agencies, Lindale, Texas.

CHAPTER 7

1 Sheila Gethaiga Kibuka at the International Conference on Children at Risk, Oxford Centre for Mission Studies, Oxford, January 1997.
2 In a paper presented to an internal WEC conference on the Fulbe in Banjul, The Gambia, September 1997.

RESOURCES

UNREACHED PEOPLES

To follow up on the work among the unreached peoples in the Sahel, try these web sites:

//www.ad2000.org
>This is the AD2000 and Beyond Movement's website. AD2000 seeks to network Christian ministries together with the aim of 'A Church for every people, and the gospel for every person' by the end of 2000.

//www.christian-info.com
>This is the site of the 'Christian Information Network' which seeks to be the 'prayer track' of AD2000.

//www.bethany-wpc.org
>Here you can find profiles of the world's least-reached peoples, including those of the Sahel. As I write this you can download individual profiles for free, or purchase a printed copy of all of them.

//www.brigada.org
>Describes itself as 'a system of conferences and forums that allow you to network with others who share common interests in sharing God's love with previously unreached cities and peoples around the world.' So you can keep up with news and discussion (admittedly of varying quality).

//www.missionnet.org
>Here you can sign up for mailing lists related to news about missions or prayer requests.

//www.woyaa.com claims to be 'Africa's search engine.' Organized by the

Churches of Christ, it has links to mission reports and news sources.

//www.africanews.org is a press agency source for African news stories.

NEWS OF THE CHURCH

For news of the Church you could try these sources:

Compass Direct
This press agency produces excellent reporting on the church in difficult or persecuted settings worldwide – in-depth, first-hand, eye-opening stuff. To subscribe, contact compassdr@compuserve.com

The *Bulletin* of The Institute for the Study of Islam and Christianity
This is a widely read and well-informed source that covers Christian issues throughout the Islamic world. Address: St Andrew's Centre, St Andrew's Road, Plaistow, London, UK E13 8QD.
Phone: 44 171 473 0743
Fax: 44 171 511 4874.

World Pulse
Published by the Evangelism and Missions Information Service of the Billy Graham Center at Wheaton College, this is a bimonthly 8-page newspaper, mostly made up of missions-related world news snippets. Address: PO Box 794, Wheaton, Ill 60189, USA.
Phone: 1-630-752-7158
Fax: 1-630-752-7155
Email: Pulsenews@aol.com

//www.religiontoday.com
Here you can find a (free) searchable archive of brief church-related news stories on many countries.

FOR PRAYER

For the Church: Paul's prayer for the Philippians seems apt: 'That your love may abound more and more in knowledge and depth of insight, so that you may be able to discern what is best and may be pure and blameless until the day of Christ, filled with the fruit of righteousness that comes through Jesus Christ, to the glory and praise of God' (Philippians 1:8–11). It covers the great calls on the large existing Christian community in West Africa: love, knowledge, insight, righteousness.

For the unreached peoples of the Sahel. There are so many of them, large and small, and they are so neglected by the Church.

For the multi-coloured church and mission force that is trying to bring the gospel to these peoples. Christian workers face a very tough life, especially in rural situations. Health, climate, and spiritual opposition all take their toll. Educating missionaries' children is a special problem here.

For the cities: that Christ will be honoured and churches established and built up.

For all those who are seeking to reduce poverty and solve the problems of the Sahel, whether they are government leaders, bankers, business people, or development agencies.